Her Imaginary Museum

Her Imaginary Museum

Poems by

Pamela Hobart Carter

Cover design by Shay Culligan
Cover art by Omar Willey
Poet photograph by Malya Hirshkowitz

ISBN: 978-1-952326-65-3

Kelsay Books
502 South 1040 East, A-119
American Fork, Utah, 84003

Dedicated to my art historian parents:

Louise Belknap Carter

and

David Giles Carter

Acknowledgments

Thank you to the editors and publishers of the following publications where these poems first appeared or are forthcoming.

Barrow Street: "Shooting at the Keeper"

The Bengaluru Review: "Pregnant," "Self-Portrait, Nude"

The Big Windows Review: "Unicorn/Gumball Machine"

The Chrysanthemum Anthology: "We Dream of the Dead and They Are Not Dead"

The Ekphrastic Review: "When Date Night Includes the Seattle Art Museum Curator's Talk, 'The Enigma of an Exalted Monk'"

Fly on the Wall Press, Chaos: "Blink"

The Museum of Northwest Art: "Mother Color," "Without Knowing"

Poetry Pacific: "A Too-Large Face"

Proem: "Unbound," "What the Viewer Understands"

The Seattle Star: "Fried Egg on the Plate, without the Plate," "Lines of Sight Are Reversible," "Puppies and Goblets," "Yearning," "Yourself, Yolk"

Contents

When Date Night Includes
the Seattle Art Museum Curator's Talk,
"The Enigma of an Exalted Monk"

Although we bolt the pot de crème
at the Thai place to run across First Avenue
in time for the museum lecture, I linger
(mentally) over the dark chocolate's bitterness
and the whipped fluff's sweetness yet grab
the juicy strawberry halves splayed at the lip
of the plate (can't bear to leave behind
their luscious redness—almost drinkable flesh
after the stiffer texture of the custard),
and we pitch ourselves, as I swallow the fruit,
together, laughing, out onto the wet walkway, dash
to make the light, and race into the packed auditorium.
In synchrony we slide into our row,
shed our warm layers, mute our phones,
and give our attention to the image
of the Chinese figure we have long loved,
known as "Monk at the Moment of Enlightenment."
(Every time we visit him, we wonder at the wild vortex
of his robe, the elation of his expression. He is in motion
and about to sing or yell.) But our curator reveals
he is someone unfamiliar, a Luohan or an Arhat,
a Dragon Catcher without his bowl or pearl.
His wooden skull, carved seven centuries ago, contains
no items of consecration—no sacred scroll,
no Yuan banknote, no semi-precious stone—
but paper chambers
encasing mummified mud wasps.

The night's incidents and fresh facts collide,
and from their crash, craft
(in our own fat-filled minds)
crackling new synapses
all the jouncy bus ride home.

Halls Never Built

No guards. No sound
except floorboards
under her feet.

The viewer, alone
in the gallery.
Paintings aglow.

Curators mounted track lighting
to perfection. Every artists' palette
richer here than ever
on their own easels—
pigments more vivid
even than in their inner visions.

The viewer walks and walks
as if hunting for Mona Lisa
at the Louvre.

But this museum
has never met a da Vinci
or a Cassatt or an ancient Greek urn.

This still labyrinth belongs
only to the viewer.

You know why.
It happens to you, too.

You have roved halls never built.
You have dug for treasures never buried.
You have sung songs never composed.

A Too-Large Face

Inspired by Echo *by Jaume Plensa*

It is how we think of childhood
and death, paler

than their awful selves, tall
versions when they are taller,

interfering more with cirrus
and icy jet trails,

when it is in simple actions
such as sliding a book

from a shelf marked *fiction*
or stacking delicious impending purchases

on the counter by the cash register,
the heart stops

and worlds fail and how
it is—my end, yours—

becomes as obvious
as a too-large face

we must admit daily
is familiar and in need of attention

Yearning

I do not want to be
remembered for my urine.
In this, I differ from
the chowchow and Welsh corgi
who yearn to soak the earth,
to imbue the foggy air,
with their unique pee scents,
who nose through the streets in search
of smells of dogs gone by,
and recorded for canine
history until rain
rinses hydrant and trunk.
If only I could so shed
skin or salt tear as I
tread my neighborhood and thus
plant in friends' hearts my deeds,
my ways, my thinking, my art—
civil equivalent
of dogs' liquid legacy.

Mother Color

Inspired by the art of Joan Kirkman
After Ursula K. Le Guin

Mother color, omnipresent, multitudinous,
descanting across canvases
in upswelling umbers, ambers, ochres, roar
of iris indigoes, mimic of Kandinsky pinks and greens,
enchantment of chartreuse ruses,
and minor scales of royal blues:
surround us. Synchronize us
with your immeasurable emissions
to hum, to hear, to harmonize,
to respect all prisms in our eyes.

Unicorn/Gumball Machine

She eyes the red ball, her eye an ebony orb, bigger
than the shiny gumball. Its neighbors—blue, green, violet,
and yellow spheres—gleam inside the clear glass tank
like giant grains of aquarium sand, lustrous. The coin pinched
between her square teeth drops into the slot, and her ivory horn
prods the release of the round rainbow envoy.

Glee spreads over her horsey face as the hard globes rattle,
beads on a psychedelic rosary,
and her polychrome prayers and her whinny
are answered when a single plop
and clattering roll signal her wished-for gift
has slid into the chute for her chomping enjoyment.

The unicorn extracts with her soft gray lips the red gumball.
Isn't this as we would all desire, that the small worlds we eye
and imagine become those upon which we may ruminate
and inspire into ephemeral existence at our leisure
as we canter deeper and deeper
into wild dark forests?

Shooting at the Keeper

Around the edges, in the emptiness,
low, or in the corner where he can't reach,
you find grace, advancement—
you know all this,
yet you fire at the keeper.

The goal lies in the negative space,
that envelops the saints adoring,
the bowls of fruit, and the Parisian café
with sky or table or a sheet of gold.
You forget you are the protagonist

and on the pitch or in a panel,
the man in the box,
framed by posts or by gilt,
draws focus—
keeper as figure; net, ground.

Our art teacher has it right
insists we see,
not laugh at, the upside-down Goya,
makes us sketch her slide of "The Third of May"
for the chance of all chances:

the formulation of a memory—
that sinister, abstracted scape broken by
white arms flung defensively toward the bottom of the screen.
Net is figure.
Keeper, ground.

What the Viewer Understands

I

There is no single line
to draw around any form,
yet our eyes describe all shapes
as if a heavy pencil defined each edge,
so the artist decides to collage
her self-portrait as realistically
as two dimensions allow.

She is, after all,
made of everything inside her body
and some of the things
in the space surrounding her movements,
and, of course, the gaseous compounds
of her respiration.

II

A strange person lives on the page built
of a daisy-filled meadow—doubtless
a few bees along with—
from a photo, which scissors have sliced
from *National Geographic.*

Between the woman illustrated,
and her location,
a wild garden spills.

III

the class understands this is realism
not visual realism
but state-of-being realism

each viewer clarifies her own presence in the world

yet a student asks why the image
only in places
has a sharp boundary between figure
and ground

the art explains
this is the truth of our existence

and further
why the head
so clear in profile of nose and mouth
opens
at the back of the skull
into sky

the art laughs
this is your reality

Without Knowing

Inspired by Dance of the Colonizers *by John Feodorov*
The Kwakwaka'wakw copper cutting ceremony may involve
breaking off a piece of copper, a symbol of wealth and alliances,
and leaving it as a challenge.

Were you pining for this invitation?

Were you altered by the entering?

Were you squeamish at the showpiece smiling?

Were you gasping at a classic's crassness?

Were you willing for a worthy history?

Were you impressed by wordless shaming?

Were you hoping for a copper cutting?

Were you unsure until the curtain?

Were you driven to remain?

Unbound

Everyone knows
the artist of this painting has been dead for centuries.

The cataloger knows
because she tracked the oil's provenance
from its day of origin,
through each of its owners,
to its current spot
on the museum wall.

The curator knows
because she has studied this artist for years and sees
everything about him this oil reveals
from its browns and ochres telling his home,
to its bold chiaroscuro
tracing his training.

The chemist knows
because he has probed
the age of the dyestuffs and varnishes.

The visitor knows
because she has traipsed
through hall after hall—
through ancient times and the middle ages
—to this oil.

While she knows
the artist is dead,
here she stands
in conversation with him.
His wit cracks her up.

Her laughter startles
the guard who is unused
to others like himself. Before opening
and after closing, he also chuckles
with the dead artist, banter unbound
by mortality or clocks.

Blue Day

Inspired by Seattle Cloud Cover *by Teresita Fernández*

Teresita Fernández
on this blue day
you give us shelter
you give us glass stratus
you give us passage
dancing day glass passage

Mesmerizer
you trap mystery in glass
tap transparencies
stratus tapestry
that daily pass
presto—in this glass

Starry Nights

Begin with night sky
above sodium-lamp city—
Ursa Major, Orion, Cassiopeia, Mars,
Venus, Moon. You have seen
what the artist saw.

Between these, stars and planets
of her own fabrication
drip off her brush—she loves
the edge of science that touches chance,
and the tempera was never to be a chart for sailors.

Infer what spaceships find.
Sketch those horse heads
and spider webs, those tufted
and tentacled bodies.

On watercolor paper, like fireworks, wet drops
of gold and green radiate. A volcano
in her imaginary galaxy erupts.
Lava spews bloody rocks
across a black expanse.

Now you have seen
what the artist dreamed.
Now you dream. Now
you see.

Fried Egg on the Plate, without the Plate

Inspired by Oeufs sur le Plat sans le Plat *by Salvador Dalí*

None of it makes sense or it all
does, doesn't matter, what matters
is how we recognize Dalí's dangling egg,
the yolk-sunny sky, and the odd shelf
as if they remind us of an impossible photo
snapped of our insides, capturing
sentiments for which we have no lyrics
only a tune by heart, same
as from a dream
or a time before birth.

Yourself, Yolk

Yourself—yolk.
Curved spine, chest-crossed arms, bare soles, curled legs—
albumen and calcareous shell.

Stiller than embryo chick sub-hen,
wait, alone. Close eyes. Render world hush.

As chick, egg-held, comes chisel-equipped;
tadpole, toothed; dancing mind will unfurl—
polliwog from slow gel.

What emerges we know for frog, fowl.

Your yolk yields idiocy, genius,
your own green glistening Athenas.

Self-Portrait, Nude

Inspired by the paintings of Paula Modersohn-Becker

The green backdrop,
is not a forest—
not a wall decorated
with paper, but color,
such that she is never
indoors or out,
but forever of paint, forever
smiling at you and herself.

Around her undressed neck
she wears a string of yellow.
The loop drapes her chest.
She smiles at you, who,
when she painted, was herself.
But she did paint for you,
she had so much to tell.

Pregnant

This painting gives birth to baby paintings,
not pretend or metaphoric births,
litters of miniatures which tumble
from the untidy backside of the canvas
where the artist stapled the edges of cloth to wood.

Trained on the gravid frame, cameras splutter
to uselessness, recording nothing of the repeating miracle.

After each phone call from the night guards,
the museum director purrs to opera
on her car radio during her inbound commute.
Ah! The institution's income is secure!
At auction, by Sotheby's, the miniatures will be gobbled up.

The subject of the painting, no surprise,
is the smiling nude self-portrait by none other
than Paula Modersohn-Becker, pregnant.
For decades art historians believed the opus
among those destroyed by Nazis.

In neglected museum storage,
a persistent cataloger, sorting through a clutch
of small unsigned pieces, had discovered,
hovering above them in the shadows,
the object of fecundity.
The complete simplicity, the simple completeness,
said it was Paula's. Her *P M-B* in the corner, surplus.

The young cataloger performed her job,
documented the crowd of little portraits of infants.

Only when Paula's pregnant nude graced
the gallery wall, and the next births occurred,

did the cataloguer attribute the nursery of tiny pictures
to the "Workshop of Paula Modersohn-Becker."

Had all these ideas come to Paula before the fatal embolism,
which killed her days after her only daughter was born?

In her notoriety, the cataloger graduates to curator,
and the infant miniatures spread Paula's legacy around the globe,
each child presenting her own humor,
her own hues, yet so like her mother.

Lines of Sight Are Reversible

Inspired by a photograph by Omar Willey

Expect when facing mirrors
glimpses at infinities, sureness

of self, in this breathing state, instead, discover
bowed lattices shuttering future or past or whatever

looking glass holds and shows with its silver surface:
no person, no time, no assurance. It is a bad habit

to check every reflection for presence
as if hoping to be swept back to innocence,

but forgivable. Walls and windows play the reel
in reverse and blink in synchrony.

Because of Borges

The artist's sister-in-law adores
the short stories of Borges.
In her favorite, he concocts
a sequence of rooms,
originating with a white one,
ending with a red one,
or the other way around,
—or is it a long corridor?—
through which a person moves,
unable to perceive the shift in color,
the final space a shock.
The artist has never read Jorge Luis Borges,
but joins her sister-in-law talking of him, nonstop.

Borges's notion is fun for fiction,
but can it be constructed?
The artist buys an old farm—tobacco,
driven under by the end of smoking.
With generous monies from a Borges foundation,
she hires a chemist and an eye doctor
to compute the number of red drops
she must mix, at each step, to mask the evolutions
from human vision.
She roughs out a flat slalom
of linked rooms, each a smidgeon
redder than the one before.

But don't we find what we foresee?
Don't we foresee what we think we know?
Visitors must stumble into the Borges …
a corn maze on one side, a haunted house
for Halloween on the other!—
billed together, at the nearby college,
as an escape from midterm memorizing.

The artist plants the kernels and converts
the old barn into something spooky.

By the midway point, she's able to score
extra funding, knowing exactly how many boards
and how much paint to order.
She also knows how many hours
remain of spraying walls, ceilings, floors.
To keep from growing bored she listens to Beethoven,
and finally, an audio of Borges, and lessons
in Mandarin, Spanish, and Portuguese.

At some moment—the effects come slowly—
the artist is stunned to find she has become
conversant in all three languages, envisions
the sheet music as she hums Beethoven, and can quote—
no, recite—all of Borges's stories.

The room-color-walk installation turns out
to be a bit of a one-liner, but popular,
especially with the philosophy professors
who add it to their course syllabi. The school bookstore
can't keep Borges in stock.

People seem not to care if they know what will come,
as the artist feared. They wish the encounter.
Repeat visitors are common—
a meditation group programs every Monday,
an auxiliary business rents headphones and recordings
of the Borges story to wear during the walk-through.

All during the next family reunion—
after the room-color-walk opens,
the artist's sister-in-law raves about Ted Chiang's "Tower
of Babylon," and the two women fall into conversation.
The artist has never heard of this author.
Her husband's sister retells Chiang's short story,
which combines Bible with historical invention,
and the artist leaves the meal full of field roast,
gravy, and dreams of high stone spirals disappearing into vapor.

Blink

How does anyone believe the artist
who says her painting will kill those who glance
without effort at its surface?

But guards keep their backs to the work all shift
and those who purchase tickets sign waivers.
Without a death, the opus travels three sites.

Critics ask, if threatened, might viewers at last
give artists their due? Is the painting a boon
to more than its venues? Is "No Blinking" the fugu of visual art?!

While the painting reminds the director
of a certain annoying childhood game,
he prohibits minors entry to the exhibit.

"No Blinking" may never be in private hands—
owners forget to value their goods, and their babies
cannot know to avert their curious tiny eyes.

The postcards, safe to glimpse, bore everyone.
Without its menace, the staring face
is a simple bully with a single skill. Plus

the brushwork is clumsy, the figure
unconvincing. The painting, a young girl sees,
is, itself, a bully.

Dismissed—a fraud?—worse?—a bully, herself?
—a gimmicker?—a gimcracker?—the artist
takes a cigarette lighter to "No Blinking."

Although quick to spray flame-suffocating foam,
the noble guard is too slow to stop her.
The painting burns to ash.

The artist adopts an alias, moves to another country,
and cultivates wine grapes (that cannot mind
being told what to do).

To admit mistakes overwhelms some of us.
We must torch everything.
Start again.

Every Guest Is Painting

An airy ballroom, half glass conservatory

dropped into a frangipani copse.

Somewhere I've never flown.

Sugar-white walls hang

with spare canvases of peach- and plum-colored birds in flight.

A little boy whose name I forget runs to sit in my lap.

Beside me, Betty, in a curly-haired wig

that clashes with her personality.

Trumpets blare.

Trolleys clatter over glazed tile

to bring wedding guests painting supplies.

Onto the pictures, as invited by the bride's father,

we swish brushes.

Jungles of jade foliage manifest,

like wetted magic scenes in children's coloring books.

(Secret messages perched

in the emptiness around air-born parrots and macaws.)

Of course, Bet is dead. That boy is in college.

And the bride's father is someone known to me.

But who was getting married?

A few brushes were more ordinary.

The party thought only to depict feathered things and trees.

Puppies and Goblets

Inspired by Still Life with Three Puppies *by Paul Gauguin*
For Omar Willey, who provided the final quotation

Look at the waggly contour
of the puppies plunked
above dark blue goblets—
sentinels between an assortment of pears,
etcetera, all on a backdrop, off-white
and decorated in a floral motif.
Who knows if Gauguin hoped
to come across as if apprenticed
to a Japanese printmaker or as a jokester
enjoying a juxtaposition
of fragile drinking vessels with squirmy spaniels?

But Van Gogh did expose his interest to his friend.
See where it got them and us?
Their paintings waiting in silent galleries.
Their time of overlap in the 1880s pondered.
Our despair lifted for a few minutes
while we study on our desktops this photo
shared by MoMA. I am almost laughing
at the perfect depiction of the little dogs.
Bellies round. Tiny tails pointing up jauntily.
Hear them slurp at their water bowl, insatiable?

The silliness of placing the litter on a table
or the glasses on the floor is delicious—
this proximity fixed in oils, for eternity.
For safety's sake the artist probably
went at each subject single-file, and tricks us

by having lain them in one frame
as if they were of the same instant,
but it "is about the sequence: how one image
combines with another, how time passes…"

We Dream of the Dead and They Are Not Dead

You emailed about your dream—
the old boyfriend
appears for casual conversation at the rural home
of our grandparents, but he is dead.
Killed himself some years ago.
Dream minds don't care about death.

We can talk to anyone
when we dream. And they are not
dirt-covered or ghostly or
the least bit decayed. They wear
khakis and button-downs and sandals
because they are in the countryside.

Their skin looks like our own browns
and pinks and they tell us no
special secrets about what lies beyond.
Then his head vaporizes.

Dead and headless old boyfriends sit,
like regular folk, in rattan chairs,
in our dreams. Their heads reappear,
if we keep talking, and may look
more insect-y, big blinkless eyes
on stalks. Perhaps no mouth?

Through his metamorphoses
though, he remains himself. In my own dreams
I've heard my mother-in-law's voice, absent
from waking life more than a decade
and, the other night, hugged our grandfather
who died when I was in grad school.

Oh, sister, our dreams can be so good
to us, even if a little Dalí-esque.

They say, *See, he is living still.*
See, he is forever in your cells.
Find him there whenever you sleep.

About the Author

Pamela Hobart Carter earned two degrees in geology from Bryn Mawr College and Indiana University before becoming a teacher. Her poems have been published by *Barrow Street, Fly On The Wall Press, Halcyon, Parks & Points & Poems, Pidgeonholes, The Seattle Times,* and *Tilde,* among others. Her poem, "Hiking to Red Pass," was nominated for a Pushcart Prize. With Arleen Williams, she is the author of twelve short books in easy English for their No Talking Dogs Press. Her plays have been read or produced in Montreal (where she grew up as a landed immigrant), Seattle (where she lives), and Fort Worth (where she has only visited). Both of Carter's parents were art historians. Sporadically, she joins other visual artists for figure drawing sessions at Seattle Ink and Oil.

www.ingramcontent.com/pod-product-compliance
Lightning Source LLC
Chambersburg PA
CBHW071359090426
42738CB00012B/3175